Understanding Dogs with the
Pack Concept

Wopila waste win

(The author's dedication in Lakota language)

Understanding Dogs with the
Pack Concept

Uli Köppel

Copyright of original edition © 2008 by Cadmos Verlag GmbH,
Im Dorfe 11, 22956 Brunsbek, Germany
Copyright of this edition © 2008 by Cadmos Books, Great Britain
Translation: Andrea Höfling
Cover design and layout: Ravenstein + Partner, Verden
Photos: Uli Köppel; Thomas Brodmann, Christiane Krieger
Editorial: Dorothee Dahl, Christopher Long
Printed by: agensketterl Druckerei, Mauerbach

British Library Cataloguing in Publication Data
A catalogue record of this book is available from the British Library.

Printed in Austria

ISBN 978-3-86127-958-7

www.cadmos.co.uk

Contents

(Photo: Köppel)

PROLOGUE

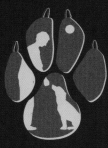

The human and his dog – the epitome of friendship and trust? Or: The human and his dog – the epitome of brutality, martyrdom and oppression?

No other animal has lived in such close proximity to humans for millennia. There is no other animal that has been adored and loved, and hated and kicked about, as much as the dog. Is it perhaps because he is so close to us, and because you can draw conclusions about a human by looking at his dog? But maybe it is his origins that are to blame; his ancestor, the wolf, who is the subject of numerous myths and fairy tales, is branded as evil and a child-eater by some, while being revered as good and even holy by others.

In order to be able to understand this special relationship, we should consider our attitude to the whole of the natural world. In a bygone age, there were more humans who saw themselves as part of nature, living with nature. They offered nature the necessary respect because they knew that they could not survive without her. This applied to all aspects of nature: the ground, the water and the entire range of fauna. Humans even turned to nature for advice, particularly from animals. To this day, many peoples still consider certain animals to be holy. But as technical progress and urbanisation advanced, people started losing their orientation on nature. With the spreading of intellectual 'enlightenment', according to which one should only believe in things that could be seen and were quantifiable, the spiritual and naive (in the sense of honest simplicity) heritage was lost, and with it the knowledge about animals. In the old days, it was well known that in a dog you were dealing with a predator, a seizer of prey who had to be treated as such. Nowadays, he often has to make up for all sort of deficits,

being used as an object for sport and utility, and even as a surrogate child or partner.

We have to return to the roots and see our dogs as dogs, and nothing else, to see them as they are: emotionally, socially and intellectually highly developed, but with reference to their own species. We have to stop 'training' them in an exploitative manner with a view to utility that stultifies them in the process. Relationship training is much more than a collection of methods and techniques for the training of dogs. It is an inner attitude, the readiness to enter a new communicative plane with a highly social animal. The dog has to be able to realise that we understand his language, as well as his needs as a pack animal, and that he is in good hands in this mixed pack with we two-legged creatures that are, after all, alien to his species. Then the first sentence of this prologue would have an exclamation mark instead of a question mark!

One should begin to treat dogs as dogs from the time they are puppies, in order to develop a species-appropriate relationship with them. (Photo: Köppel)

The human and his responsibility

Looking at the 'dog scene' of our day, it is striking to see how confused and confusing it has become of late. It almost seems like a new book about dogs is being published every other day – each, of course, propagating a revolutionary new method, purporting to be based exclusively on 'well-founded' theories about learning. Even if most of these 'new methods' are old hat, who cares? Sporting an upbeat layout, and endorsed by 'dog trainers' who are mostly good at marketing themselves, many of these books have become bestsellers.

Upon further investigation, however, it quickly turns out that the respective styles of dog training are in complete contradiction with each other; and you, as a dog owner, who only wants the best for his dog, are supposed to make sense of all this confusion!

At the same time, hardly a week goes by in which there isn't a mauling incident being reported by the press, or at least some kind of negative event regarding the relationship between human and dog – not to mention the dogs who 'just want to play' and who will jump up at you as you are jogging, cycling or hiking past, while barking insecurely, or who may even take a snap at your posterior.

The first rule must be that a dog, no matter how big or small, should never become a risk to humans. We are not just talking about maulings. If your dog does not wholly accept you as his pack leader, and as a consequence you are not able to control him at all times, then this is already a precarious state of affairs. Such a dog will determine what he will do next with reference only to himself. Even if he 'only' runs to meet a dog friend of his, which involves him having to cross the road, there is a great risk of an accident. This is only one of many examples. Supposedly, the dog is meant to be our friend and partner who accompanies us wherever we go! He can only do this if, from his perspective, everything regarding his pack is well in order.

Upbringing inside the pack

The reason why there are so many badly behaved dogs (despite the number of dog schools that seem to have sprung up all over

Dogs possess a highly social family system and system of upbringing. Let's emulate the father dog in order to enable a harmonious relationship between dog and human to develop. (Photo: Köppel)

the place) is simply the conveniently forgotten truth that there is a predator attached to the other end of the leash. This predator of the canidae family, as he is known in scientific terms, has to be brought up in the same way as he would have been with his original family in the pack. The methods used by the pack are: play-based learning, species-appropriate disciplining, tabooing and benign consistency.

In order to bring up a dog in a species-appropriate manner, we don't need any exploitative utility-related training, but rather an emotional relationship that is based on these foundations. Whether you are bringing up a puppy or you have an older dog, the only way to develop a species-appropriate relationship based on what the dog is asking of you, and therefore understands, is to be prepared to take the responsibility of thinking and acting like a dog.

This is why every dog owner, and those wishing to become one, should be aware of their responsibility.

Why do I want a dog in the first place?

That is, admittedly, a self-critical question: why do I want a dog in the first place? Or, to put it another way: have I actually got what it takes for this responsible task? This means only those who are sure that they don't want a designer object to add to their chic home and model family (possibly even a expensive model of the currently trendy dog breed, without regard to compatibility), and those who don't need to satisfy a neurotic need to fuss over, to overfeed and overindulge, without any regard for the dog's needs. You should ask yourself this question just as seriously as you should ask yourself which breed and which size dog will really be compatible with your family, your flat, and your experience.

Collect your puppy at the age of eight weeks in order to be able to make the best of the all-important socialising phase in regard to your dog's upbringing. (Photo: Köppel)

In the socialisation phase, a dog learns that it is better to act as part of a team rather than to act in a selfish manner. (Photo: Köppel)

The right time for taking a puppy home

The next question is: when is the right time to collect a puppy from the breeder? There are increasing numbers of breeders, especially those breeding the larger breeds, who, as a rule, will only hand over their puppies after the age of twelve weeks. Their argument is that the puppies ought to spend the socialisation phase between the eighth and the twelfth week of life with their mother, and in their familiar surroundings. This would offer them the opportunity to realise their awakening urge to play and scamper about in the company of their littermates, and as a result they will be more mature by the time they arrive in their new home.

Looking at it from a behaviourist perspective, you will arrive at a different conclusion.

In the pack, the mother dog will invariably hand over the puppies to the father around the eighth week. The puppies quickly accept this change in circumstances without any problem, a fact that can easily be ascertained, because from that moment onward they will eagerly follow in their father's wake, instead of their mother's, even though she is still their primary source of food. Because most breeders don't keep male dogs – and, in any case, most certainly not the father of the puppies – this natural process cannot take place. This means the mother is forced to take on the father's role to the best of her ability. As a consequence, at this stage of their development the puppies have to form a renewed bond with their mother, even though their biological parameters are set to experience this with the other parent. Then after week twelve they are handed over to their new owner. Thinking of these natural processes, it can easily be imagined what a deep impact on the dog's psyche this represents.

The conclusion: nature has prepared dogs for a separation in their eighth week of life, and, rather sensibly, this is also the time when their nervous system can withstand the most stress. Hence this is clearly the best time for them to move to a new home.

The second important argument is that the above-mentioned socialisation phase takes place between the eighth and the twelfth weeks.

At this point I'd like to clear up a widespread misconception: the 'socialisation phase' does not mean that you have to expose your puppy's senses to an ever increasing number of new and strange impressions and stimuli, as is being suggested in many puppy schools.

No, its primary function in the pack is to teach the puppy how to transform himself into a social being, a part of a team. The father dog plays an important part in this. He demonstrates to his charges through species-appropriate play that togetherness and teamwork offer fun and pleasure, and lead to a collective experience of success. This is the elementary basis for the successful survival of the pack in the face of the hardships of nature. A change of owners at this point means that the human enters a puppy's life as the most important personality, taking the place of the father dog. If we want to do everything right from the start, we will accept this position with all it involves, proving to be a 'father dog' who is one hundred per cent dependable!

The puppy will give us his trust, which we must not disappoint under any circumstances by not relating to his needs. So we will offer him something he would expect from the adult dog as well: play-based learning! Exactly how this is going to work will be discussed later, but for now let's have a look at how a dog actually thinks.

How does an
intact dog
brain think?

In a sense, it works in a very similar way to ours. There are many parallels between bringing up a dog and bringing up children – provided you really do want to bring up your child by leading with your own example and offering the necessary consistency.

If you were a follower of the ideas of laissez-faire, however, I'd advise against you getting a dog. Dogs, like children need clearly defined structures and limits. Only with these in place are they able to develop and thrive, only then do they know they are safe and well.

Bringing up a dog has a lot in common with bringing up children. Both parties need very defined structures and limits. Dogs have to develop their individuality in order to be able to become socially intelligent dogs. (Photo: Köppel)

The father dog shows us how it's done. Puppies and juvenile dogs need a boss who knows his stuff.
(Photo: Köppel)

This is because the freedom to develop socially and emotionally can only be safeguarded if there are clearly defined limits. Be a role model for your dog.

Give him clear taboos, and use them to practise a benign consistency. Be ready to act if your dog transgresses a taboo in spite of this! Ignoring a transgression is not an option; in the pack, this simply doesn't exist. (In case you still think that the ignoring method has any merit, please try it out on your child. Next time he's pinched a bar of chocolate from the cupboard and eaten it, despite you having told him not to, just ignore it. You'll be very likely to achieve an educational success by this...)

Species-appropriate disciplining

No, your dog expects something different: species-appropriate disciplining! This doesn't mean you should give him a hiding with a rolled-up newspaper or an umbrella; dogs in a pack don't have that sort of thing. Rather, take him by the scruff of his neck and give him a brief shake. It is important you do this with the deepest conviction and with full-on emotion. You don't have to shout or scream, as unfortunately is often the case at many dog schools. No, on the contrary, all you need to do is to be completely sure of yourself. Here again, you

Practising species-appropriate upbringing means that we have a solid relationship with our dog.
(Photo: Köppel)

can see similarities with child rearing. A strong will and emotion should not be confused with despotic behaviour and hysterical screaming. All our dogs want is to know consistently where they stand, and where their taboos and limits are. If you have a puppy that you are bringing up in a species-appropriate manner, non-verbal disciplining will soon become obsolete. If you are dealing with an older dog, it may take a little longer until he has understood and accepted that you are now the head of the pack. After that, verbal disciplining is usually enough to put everything to rights again. Dogs are very good observers by nature; they instantly register any inconsistency on our part, and they will test us, no matter whether they are puppies, juveniles or adult dogs. A dog that has been brought up in a species-appropriate manner will later generously forgive you the occasional slip-up, because he knows that otherwise everything is in good order.

The human as the dog's role model

Even if in the dog scene terms like 'alpha wolf', 'leader of the herd' or 'boss of the pack' are being questioned these days, a dog needs a human who will serve as his role model.

He is literally looking out for this. Of course, this should not be confused with a totalitarian tyranny. Nor does it mean that in order to prove his dominant position the human always has to be the first to walk through doors and gates, or that the dog must not be allowed on to the first floor of the house, because that would elevate him above his humans. This sort of thing only enters the minds of those who don't know much about dogs. Dogs possess a very pronounced ability to think. They have a highly social and differentiated pack structure, a highly developed brain with the ability for logical thought, and an excellent memory. Nevertheless, your dog won't necessarily think in the way you might like him to, or like in those idealising representations that endow dogs with human traits. He will always think like a dog. That's why it is your responsibility as a dog owner to provide him with what he needs: a species-appropriate upbringing and thoughtful leadership.

If you don't, you'll end up in the dilemma of the 'social agreement', which is a term I like to use. A dog owner who has such a 'social agreement' with his dog can be recognised by this standard statement: 'My dog is basically obedient, but…' Or another one: 'I'll just have to distract him with a treat, and then put him on his leash…'. Dogs such as these will occasionally mark the armrests of the mother-in-law's sofa, or empty the neighbours' bin while you're there on a visit. You can complete this list yourself…

A dog who isn't taking his master or mistress seriously, because he quite rightly doesn't regard them as proper pack leaders, will do as he pleases – sometimes even obey, when he doesn't happen to have anything else on his mind. In approximate terms he is thinking about his humans as follows: 'They are really nice people from whom I can get my stroking units whenever I like, and on top of that they are great tin-openers; but alas, they are not leadership material!'

The dog in a surrogate pack – the family

This state of affairs can become unpleasant and even risky when the dog lives in a family, especially if the children are still small. If they view the dog as an in-house petting zoo, or an object on which to vent their aggressions, you may end up with a serious problem on your hands. Most dogs will be happy to integrate the human offspring lovingly into the human-dog pack, but in return they expect from us, the pack bosses, that we teach our children how to deal with the other pack members in an appropriate manner. Otherwise, if there is no pack boss around to discipline the child, our dog will do the job instead at the next available opportunity, and he would be within his rights to do so.

Imagine the following everyday situation. You have just told off your child because the rubbish bin, which he was supposed to have emptied, remains unemptied in the kitchen. The child stomps off to his room in a huff, meets the dog in the hall, and in passing vents his anger on him by giving his ear a good tug.

Our dog will be completely taken aback at first. But at the next opportunity he will explain to this prepotent pack member, in dog terms, that this is not the way things are done around here, by taking a defensive snap at him, or even gripping him lightly with his teeth. The result is a great wringing of hands on the part of the family. The dog may possibly be classified as 'aggressive', even though from his perspective he has absolutely done the right thing; and he may be taken to a dogs' home or even put to sleep. If the dog is fortunate enough to be living with sensible human beings, neither of these things will happen, because the parents would analyse the situation and look for the root cause of the problem.

As you can see, it really is not an easy task for human beings to take responsibility for a dog, albeit a very life-enriching one. Everyone who takes their dog seriously and wants him by their side as a trusting partner will be able to confirm this.

Develop-mental phases

Without exceeding the remit of this book, I would like to deal briefly with the dog's developmental phases, because I'll only be able to fine-tune the relationship with my dog to the optimum degree, if on one hand, I know how the whole thing would unfold in nature, and on the other, the meaning and purpose of these developmental stages.

I will mention the first three phases only for the sake of completing the picture, because we are (in most cases) not able to influence them. It's a different story for those who breed dogs themselves. The first two weeks of a dog's life are called the vegetative phase, because the puppies are still completely deaf and blind.

From the third week onwards begins the interim phase. During this time the puppies open their eyes for the first time, with their acoustic sense also awakening. In addition, at this time the first, albeit purely instinctive, contact with their litter-mates is made. The fourth week of life already has a great influence on the puppy's further development, as this is when the imprinting phase begins. As the name suggests, everything that is imprinted – or not imprinted, as the case may be – will become an indelible part of the dog's behavioural inventory. This is also the moment when his eagerness to learn and his instinct for imitation awaken. This developmental stage ends around the eighth week of life.

The socialisation phase, which is of fundamental importance for the dog's later life, begins in the eighth week. (Photo: Köppel)

The socialisation phase

The socialisation phase begins at the eighth week of life. This phase represents the great point of access for we dog owners to begin working on the relationship with our dog, and at the same time to start the species-appropriate upbringing. As we have seen already, in nature this is the point at which the father takes over the puppies' upbringing to become social and useful pack members. Now it is up to us to take over the responsibility for this task.

We are laying the foundations for a peaceful future life together. During this stage of his development, the dog learns what he is allowed to do and what he is not allowed to do. At the same time, we show the puppies with the use of tabooing that we are more experienced than them. This, together with species-appropriate disciplining, enables us to build physical and psychological authority. The father dog puts a lot of emphasis on play-based learning, while at the same time insisting on the strict adherence to certain rules; for example, the point at which a game is ended, or continued with a different object. We simply do exactly the same.

At this point, we begin with species-appropriate, play-based learning. This could be the concentration exercise 'sit' (see Basic training: the concentration exercise 'sit'). Also very suitable are tug-of-war games, or those involving 'prey'. Take an old cloth, or something similar, and begin to play with this 'prey'. If your puppy gets really wrapped up in the game and starts to pull with gusto, and even growls a little, this is great. But make sure you don't always pull in your direction; you should also give in to your dog's efforts every now and then. When you want to end the game use words such as 'Let go', so that the dog learns to give up the 'prey'. Afterwards, just walk away from him or let him keep the 'prey'. Don't worry: this won't diminish your authority in any way, as is often claimed. The important thing is that you are the one who determines the duration of the playing session.

This is how to develop a species-appropriate relationship with your charge, involving an upbringing in a real dog-specific sense, instead of so-called 'training' which is stultifying for your dog and for you. If you collect your dog from the breeder at eight weeks old and undertake this species-appropriate educational programme, you are offering the dog exactly the same thing that he would have in his natural surroundings: an intact pack with you as the boss who takes charge of the dog's 'further education'. Your puppy will realise that you, although alien to his species, are the same as or, in an intellectual sense, superior to the father dog, and that you will therefore do everything in your power to keep strengthening your mutual emotional bond's invisible ties.

The pecking order phase starts from the thirteenth week onwards. It is specially designed for the observation of clearly structured limits. (Photo: Köppel)

The pecking order phase

With the thirteenth week of a puppy's life, a new developmental stage is about to begin: the pecking order phase. As the name suggests, what is being learned and practised here is the observation of a clearly defined order throughout the whole pack. Contrary to what the name suggests, however, among dogs this doesn't work in the same way as the primitive pecking order practised among chickens, for example. No, what we can see here is a very complex form of a social hierarchy within the pack. In a very small pack, the pack order is clearly structured from the onset; parents, juveniles and puppies automatically form a hierarchy. It's different with larger family groups. They roughly share the same structure with the small pack, with the difference that the subdivisions of adult dogs, juvenile dogs and puppies are structured individually, as well. With this definition, every subdivision makes its social contribution to form a viable pack.

It is comparable to a football team. Here, too, you have several goalkeepers, defenders, midfield players and centre forwards. Everybody wants to occupy their own proper place. Depending on which system the trainer (boss) is subscribing to, the players have to take the position assigned to them, in order to play their part in the collective to the optimum effect. During the pecking order phase, our dogs represent the young players who will one day play in the position assigned to them by their trainer.

The pecking order phase has two important functions. The first is a second sifting out of juvenile dogs with possible genetic or health defects. These would primarily manifest themselves during feeding. As the bosses emphasise their privileged position during feeding, the underbosses do the same on the lower rungs of the hierarchy. The same can be observed among juvenile dogs. Consequently a juvenile dog who is sickly or instinctually challenged would not achieve a feeding position that would enable him to survive in the long run.

The second, and in my view the rather more fundamental function, is practising the jockeying for positions in a playful manner. If the socialisation phase means that the time has begun to learn about species-appropriate play, e.g., catching games, fighting and tug-of-war games, in the pecking order phase these increase in intensity, and may even assume a slightly aggressive note. It goes without saying that the aggression is not real. It's only about setting their increasingly awakening motor skills against each other, in order to find a position in the subpack of adolescents. I am always

We also have to observe our dog's facial expression very closely in order to act appropriately. Juvenile dogs in particular will try to test us, unless we are clear and consistent. (Photo: Köppel)

reminded of my own time at school, where you would find a pecking order among the pupils, created by pushing and shoving, running off or running after others. Everybody wanted to be the boss's best friend.

During this developmental stage, the father dog also continues to work consistently at being recognised in his authority. He demonstrates this by intervening in the fight games, and interrupting them every now and then. The measures at his disposal for this purpose range from level one to three. The first level is simply entering the presence of the competing juvenile dogs. For some, this is already sufficient cause for interrupting their game, in order to show their father the required reverence. For the slightly more thick-skinned charges, who don't display this behaviour straightaway, a piercing look and a slight to medium growl is added. The third and ultimate level is reserved for the really hard-boiled cases in the adolescent pack. The father dog will take disciplining measures, thus claiming his right to have the ultimate say.

Here the question arises of how this situation will pan out regarding our relationship with our dog. Has the puppy or juvenile dog accepted you as the pack boss yet? If you are able to recall your dog from playing with other dogs without any problems, you may answer this question with a resounding yes. You will also know the answer by simply looking at your dog. A well-adjusted juvenile dog is balanced, because although curious and lively, he has, after all, a secure base to fall back on. With you as his surrogate father on two legs to support him, he can explore his surroundings with a sense of trust and security, and he will be able

to develop and thrive. Just to make this quite clear, the 'father dog' on two legs can, of course, be female as well. We're only dealing with an 'official title' here!

If we offer our juvenile dog what he is expecting of us during this period, he will show his enthusiasm towards us time and time again. Just as in a proper dog pack, he will prove his loyalty and allegiance by displaying emotional devotion and affection. You have to allow your juvenile dog to do this from time to time, and don't reject him. Enter into physical contact with your dog by sitting, or lying down next to him, allowing him to carry out the ritual of belonging in the proper manner, with his tongue to be precise – and preferably in your face. Then you know that everything's just fine on both sides.

Konrad Lorenz once coined the term 'allegiance' for this behaviour. This basically alludes to the fact that there are no generational conflicts within a dog pack, because no young rowdy would ever dream of mounting any opposition against the adult dogs or questioning their leadership competence. The youngsters have everything they need for a healthy growing-up process: clearly defined structures providing a sense of security, the feeling of being looked after and belonging, and proper limits that indicate to them what is allowed and what is not. Ultimately, this way they have the greatest possible freedom for their development as individuals.

Keeping all that in mind, the tremendous significance of the pecking order phase, and the great opportunities it offers, will become obvious. If we emulate the work that goes on within the dog pack, regarding upbringing and relationships, we will achieve our desired goals. Our dog will increasingly respect our emotional and intellectual authority. By doing this we will achieve a natural subordination, without the stupid and useless 'subordination exercises' at dog school that would turn our dog into a neurotic slave, to say the least, instead of a four-legged partner. Learning through play during the pecking order phase remains the elementary educational tool for steadily reinforcing the invisible bond between us, and our juvenile dog. As a result, his allegiance as well as his subordination will become more and more intense. Playing with us will remain a fundamental expression of the social bond until old age. Our dog is saying to us in no uncertain terms: 'We belong together 'til death do us part.'

The pack order phase

The pack order phase is the next stage in the life of our juvenile dogs. It begins at twenty weeks and ends at about the twenty-eighth week of the dog's life. These dates can only be approximations, as it is well known that smaller dogs develop quicker in every respect than dogs who will grow to a larger size. As the name of this life stage suggests, it is, in a manner of speaking, the last piece of the puzzle on the way to achieving a well-functioning pack as a whole. The juvenile dogs are now supposed to become fully fledged family members, who will already be entrusted with certain tasks. This is the case with regard to hunting above all. The biological background for this phase is usual-

If we behave like a father dog, we are laying the foundations for the dog's orientation towards his human, which Konrad Lorenz called 'allegiance'. (Photo: Köppel)

ly the onset of autumn. There are difficult times ahead for the pack. Every paw is needed for the collective hunt. In addition, the larger prey are migrating towards more southerly regions, in order to have better access to food. This means the dogs are required to show a greater readiness to run than was necessary for summer hunting. If the pack wasn't absolutely stable and sworn to loyalty at this point, it would mean certain death for the entire clan.

For we dog owners, this is a more than an obvious hint. If we were to wait until then before starting any educational measures, biologically we would lag behind our dog, and he would vehemently rise up on his hind legs, if we were to try this – and from his perspective, rightly so. Let's not follow in the footsteps of all those 'dog-wrestlers' who won't begin the dog's upbringing properly until a year has gone by, and who then have to resort to brute force to show their dog which way the wind is blowing. You have to suspect that this is exactly what these types need in order to prop up their self-esteem.

Let's do it differently! Let's start species-appropriate upbringing from the eighth week onwards, and thus develop an emotional bond with our dog. Then we can use the pack order phase to give our relationship the last finishing touches by increasingly making use of joint play, as well as tracking and searching, each of which I have described in their own dedicated chapters later. This serves as our substitute for the collective hunt that would happen in the pack at this stage. We can cultivate the hunting dog's simultaneously emerging urge to expand his territory by jointly exploring new territory

Collective playing is a substitute for collective hunting. (Photo: Köppel)

with him. Go jogging, cycling or similar with your dog, and interrupt this activity by laying a track and searching for it together. Once the search has been concluded successfully, have a good playing session with him. This joint activity will weld you together for the whole of your dog's future life.

Give your imagination a free rein as you are thinking up new games to play together. You can vary the tracking work between a free search, where the dog is allowed to determine himself how he wants to search for the hidden object, and a track search, where he is only allowed to search following the tracks left by you. During this game, we only intervene if he has lost our tracks or has decided to leave them. This strengthens the team spirit, and our dog is one hundred per cent in his element!

Explore new territory with your dog. Using your tricycle for this purpose enables your dog to indulge in his urge to run, as well. (Photo: Köppel)

Let us make use of this pack order phase in order to reinforce those things we have already practised with our puppy. We should keep showing him new variations and nuances, because at this developmental stage our juvenile dog has a tremendous thirst for knowledge. We develop his cognitive and, above all, his social skills by offering him as many new experiences as possible. This will have a positive effect on his entire behaviour.

I'd like to mention two more things in this context: On the one hand, what will happen in almost every pack in the wild is that juvenile dogs will separate from the family group in order to try their luck with starting up their own pack. This, of course, is impossible in the symbiotic human-dog relationship. At least it ought not be possible, even though the reality of many human-dog relationships does look a bit different. In many cases, the juvenile dog makes extensive use of his 'freedom' to expand his territory by absconding or straying! As we have seen, this is an expression of our failure as dog owners to develop a species-appropriate relationship with our dog. If, on the other hand, we have managed to achieve this relationship through consistently working at it from week eight onwards, our dog would not subject us to any 'tests' at this stage, in order to question our authority. He would see no reason why he should leave this competent pack boss.

On the other hand, in a certain sense we will always remain in the pack order phase regarding our human-dog pack, because in the setting of human civilisation, we are in fact our dog's lifelong carers and supervisors. In addition, his urge to hunt and to expand his territory have to be civilised and sublimated, in order to make it possible to live together harmoniously in an urban society. At this point, at the latest, it becomes obvious that our dog does not need a 'dog trainer' or a 'fusspot auntie'. Instead he needs a human being as his boss by his side, who understands him, who will assign him a firm position in the pack, and who will use his physical and psychological authority to give him guidance and a sense of security. As a result, the dog will not have to protect a leaderless pack by taking on the position of pack leader himself. A dog who is sure of his instincts would only do this in the absence of a discernible boss, in which case, as we well know, we are in trouble…

The puberty phase

After the pack order phase one last small problem awaits us: the puberty phase. This developmental stage begins between the seventh and ninth month of our dog's life, depending on his size. A sure sign that our juvenile dog has entered this new stage of life is the lifting of the leg in the male, and the first heat in the female. Just as with human adolescents this is a time of great upheaval, if there are problems at the foundations of our home life. If solid foundations have been laid well in advance, and our juvenile dog has made the experience up to this point, that everything is in good 'dog order', this phase should not have much of an impact. Nevertheless, now and then during the puberty phase small insecurities of a social nature may occur, but normally these will disappear again on their own account, provided we don't alter our style of upbringing. They are caused by the hormonal changes, which are happening in the adolescent's body, creating havoc just as with our two-legged pubescent teenagers. Sometimes you get the feeling that the dog in front of you has never even heard of 'proper' behaviour before. Nevertheless, let's stick with the three cornerstones of species-appropriate upbringing for dogs – benign consistency, species-appropriate disciplining and tabooing – and we will survive this period without much trouble. Because the puberty phase only lasts about four to eight weeks, we can breathe a sigh of relief afterwards, and can rest assured in the knowledge that we've gained a friend for life; and in the fulness of time you'll increasingly become a well-oiled team, almost like an old married couple.

The pack order phase is followed by the puberty phase. Just like human teenagers, our dogs are subject to hormonal turmoil during this phase. (Photo: Köppel)

A question of
dominance

Once we as dog owners take responsibility, and
we want to bring up our dog in a species-appropriate manner, the question of dominance quickly
appears on the horizon. Before anything else, let
me say one thing: if you, dear reader, want to
'dominate' your dog, I'd advise you not to get a
dog in the first place. It would be just as wrong,
however, if a dog who is a predator and herd animal, was left without a pack leader among his
group. In order to avoid any misunderstandings
I would like to keep the word 'dominance' out
of canine upbringing altogether.

Dominance – a word that is usually completely misinterpreted with regard to the upbringing of dogs.
(Photo: Köppel)

Well-defined structures and clear rules

All higher developed and social beings need a well-defined structure in their family group. This is not a despotic structure, but one that is founded on experience, maturity and consistency, just as in a human family there are rules and limits that have to be respected, in order to allow the survival of the group. The following example makes this clear.

Let's assume we were living with our extended family in the wilderness. Our survival depends on each individual member of this group.

Because we have to provide for ourselves, everybody has a task, depending on talent and age. There are hunters, who provide prey for the family. After the edible parts of the prey have been prepared for food, other members of the group turn the non-edible remains into useful things. There are also people looking after agriculture and other important things. Everybody is depending on everybody else, because this is the only way of guaranteeing the extended family's survival. Just as important as the assignment of different work-related tasks is the (pecking) order within the family. For this, too, there are well-defined structures and limits. A human who is the head of the group would be this extended family's leader. He is ultimately responsible for what and how things are done. He carries the burden of all decisions great and small, and hence also the issue of the survival of the entire group. He ensures that every member adheres to the rules, and enforces this with consistency.

The group's infants automatically grow into this structure. The group's juveniles learn from the adults and accept their function as role models. They have been imbibed with the knowledge that there are taboos and limits that everybody has to stick to. Transgressions are consistently dealt with by enforcing discipline, and the use of sanctions. Only an intact family can guarantee survival!

This is what our dogs and their ancestors, the wolves, think, too. They don't need any despotic dominance from their humans, or, its opposite number, the laissez-faire attitude that abrogates any responsibility. Our dogs – like our children, by the way – need only one thing: clear rules

Instead of a misguided notion of dominance, the three cornerstones of a species-appropriate upbringing should be consistency, disciplining and tabooing. (Photo: Köppel)

that have been defined by us, the head of the pack, and which are put into practice with benign consistency and species-appropriate upbringing. They also need role models that they can trust. Only if these things are in place, is a highly developed being able to grow up in a safe and protected manner.

Our dog still carries the model of the extended family inside him, even though in our part of the world there are no longer any naturally grown dog packs living in the wild according to their own laws. He sees us as a surrogate pack, whether it consists only of the two of us, or whether there are other 'pack members', as well. For him, the main concern is for us to set him limits and rules, as well as keeping to them with consistency. If we show our dog limits and rules in a way that he can understand in the manner of his species, we will become the head of the pack, and he will respect us. For our dog, we have become the boss, without having had to resort to chastisements such as spiked dog collars, umbrellas or even electrical devices.

Consistency and disciplining

Dogs have three important basic elements in their educational programme. In position one is the benign consistency. Benign because your motivation is not the preservation of the pack leader's power, but the well-being of the whole pack. Consistency, because you will get unambiguous situations that can be understood by everybody only if you act in a consistent manner.

This is followed by species-appropriate disciplining. If a juvenile has transgressed the rules or committed a provocation, he will be disciplined, and by this reintegrated into the pack or family group. This prevents anarchy and a breaking apart of the pack. Dogs employ a number of different measures to enforce discipline, which can be applied to the human-dog interaction in the same way.

For smaller transgressions, or when dealing with very small puppies, an emotionally charged growl or a threatening snap in the direction of the perpetrator usually suffices. For you as a human, it is not really important what you say or shout, but how you do it; you have to mean what you say, and your dog has to realise that you are angry. If he respects the threatening gesture, everything is all right. In case he is less than impressed, or you are dealing with juveniles or older dogs, you have to move on to the next stage: gripping the dog by the scruff of his neck and giving him a quick shake. Where appropriate, this can be combined with throwing the dog on his back. Despite being discredited by 'modern dog education experts', because according to them the dog would misunderstand this as a 'shaking to death' (more about that later), the shaking by the scruff of the neck is, to put it simply, a basic element of disciplining used in the dog pack.

Looking at this procedure on film in super-slow motion, you can see the following. The father approaches the juvenile dog while making a lot of noise. His snout is pointing towards the juvenile dog's neck. In most cases he does not actually have to grip the scruff of the neck at all, because the delinquent will instantly make himself small and throw himself on his back. This is what the father dog had wanted to achieve, because with this the juvenile dog demonstrates active submission. The real 'shaking by the neck' can be observed mainly when the disciplined party is a bit older. Here the adult dog really does go for the scruff of the neck, thereby conveying a warning. Here, too, the aim is for the admonished dog to turn on his back, offering his active submission. If, for example, your dog were to lean too far out of the window, then you too would be allowed – or rather obliged – to demand this active submission from your dog.

Tabooing

The third important cornerstone in canine upbringing is tabooing. Taboos are vital for survival in the pack. As mentioned before, dogs have to rely on social learning for almost all important things in life. They have no innate sense to tell them whether a thing in their environment is dangerous or harmless. They are not able to tell, for example, whether a mushroom is poisonous or not, or whether this small creature here – snake, spider, scorpion – is deadly or edible. Without the intervention of educational tabooing and passing on the experience from the older to the younger generation, there soon wouldn't be any dogs left. Or, rather, we wouldn't have any dogs in the first place, because as a result of this trial and error their ancestors, the wolves would have become extinct long ago.

The measures used for disciplining and tabooing exclusively serve a single goal, which is to turn the tiny tot into a socially intelligent dog who one day may be able to lead the pack himself. In addition, the puppy and the juvenile dog know that you can rely on the experience of the older dog one hundred per cent, and that gives them security. This strengthens the spiritual-emotional bond between them. Your dog expects tabooing measures because they are part of his educational programming. When the terms dominance and discipline are mentioned in the context of species-appropriate upbringing, this has nothing whatsoever to do with what some utility-based dog schools mean by them – whether they mean the use of violence on the part of the human (no matter which implement is used) or so-called 'educational' methods for teaching the dog who's in charge, such as tethering the dog for hours on end or keeping him locked in dark cages.

Dogs have to be able to recognise clearly the limits and possibilities of a social structure. (Photo: Köppel)

The process of getting to know one another also requires clear rules being followed. (Photo: Köppel)

Disciplining means teaching puppies, and also sometimes naughty older dogs, those indispensable rules for ensuring a harmonious family life. These rules, however, always have to be adapted to the relevant situation. By doing so, neither the dog's individuality, nor his personality, is suppressed. On the contrary, he can develop freely, just learning the limits and possibilities of the social structure within which he has to find his place.

In order for the pack to remain functioning, there have to be a certain number of rules that everybody adheres to, because that is the only way to ensure the survival of the group and that of the species. Misfits haven't got a chance

here. Either they would be bitten to death one day or forever cast adrift from the pack.

At this point I'd like to touch upon an important subject: the unauthorised leaving of the pack, called 'straying' by we humans. Every time, at the same spot the rascal will run off into the distance, and you can call and shout as much as you like: he won't listen! On the contrary, he will cast a mischievous look back at you, before really turning up the speed. After a while he will return voluntarily. What's to do? Very often in dog books and at dog schools you'll get the following advice for this situation: 'Whatever you do, don't scold the dog, he would not understand it. Moreover, he would associate the scolding with the act of returning. You should rather reward him with a treat, because he has come back to you after all!'

To say it quite clearly, in the pack such unauthorised action would be punished severely.

If you think about the aforementioned necessity for everybody to be able to depend on everybody else, then it becomes obvious that such a behaviour would represent a serious danger to the pack. Only an intact pack where everyone knows their place is a safe pack.

A stray would be disciplined without fail upon his return by just about every single family member. He may even be beaten up, to make him realise that in a well-functioning family group such behaviour is not acceptable. Unless our stray happens to suffer from some sort of a genetic glitch, he will certainly never do it again.

Likewise, our dog knows that he would have to expect a species-appropriate disciplining if everything in the pack is as it is supposed to be. Dogs have highly developed cognitive abilities and an excellent memory. Without these abilities they would never able to form social groups of such complexity. Therefore dogs are well aware what they have done, and are able to suffer a 'guilty conscience'. Of course, this does not refer to some abstract norms to feel guilty about, but to clear social rules and taboos, all well known to the dog.

When you come home and find the priceless Persian rug – a gift from the in-laws – has been perforated just a little, or your dog has taken off because that rabbit was so irresistible, you should react in a species-appropriate manner by disciplining your dog. You will observe an interesting change in him!

This is what it looks like when a dog offers his submission, a gesture sometimes demanded by the father dog. (Photo: Köppel)

Species-appropriate play-based learning

We have looked at the three cornerstones of species-appropriate dog upbringing: tabooing, disciplining and consistency. If these were to remain the only components of our dog's upbringing, a very elementary part would be missing: play-based learning! This would be a great pity, not only because we would be denying the puppy the fulfilment of a basic need, but also because we would have to admit to ourselves that we are no longer able to master this ancient basic form of learning.

Play-based learning forms the basis of dog upbringing. (Photo: Köppel)

Just as it is for we humans, play-based learning is the mainstay of dog upbringing. For highly developed mammals such as dogs, their ability to acquire knowledge about social rules and agreements through play-based learning determines whether they thrive or face obliteration. In addition to the educational and knowledge-based elements, play also offers behavioural patterns for appeasing, resolving anxiety, as well as inhibiting aggression. At this point I'd like to heartily recommend everyone to read the works of Irenäus Eibl-Eibesfeldt, who has written groundbreaking and important material about this subject, as part of his contribution to behavioural science.

There is very little that is genetically predetermined, i.e., present from birth, in a social and environmentally open mammal such as the dog. This is why, strange as it may seem, he has to learn how to play. At the same time, by doing so he is able to adapt to a huge variety of environmental conditions. It is only due to this fact that dogs are able to live in such close proximity with humans. If you bear in mind how all these things correlate, you will realise how important it is for our dog to play with us. Let us take a closer look at play-based learning with regard to dogs. How do our dogs play? What do they play with? Who plays with whom? And, the most important question for us, how should we, as dog owners, play with our dog?

To put it in simple terms, dogs in the pack always play with serious intent, or rather, they don't play for the sake of playing. The primary aspect of all play consists of learning and consolidating those behaviours, social and otherwise, which are needed for later life. Each individual playing session has sections and sequences from various different chains of action and social situations built into it, which are thus practised again and again.

The motivation for play-based learning is innate in humans, just as it is in all other mammals. The dog's motivation to persevere, however, fluctuates a lot, just as it does with our children. At the beginning, canine children have trouble concentrating on one type of play and one play situation, and they will try to seamlessly switch from one playing element to another, once they get the feeling that it's going on a bit or it's too hard for them. If the male dog whose original role in the pack would be to organise this part of the upbringing had the opportunity to intervene, he would do so at exactly this point. From the eighth week of the puppies' life he would insist on his charges sticking to certain rules, regarding, for example, what they play with and how long for. He would proceed with a very individual approach, because he would know that not every puppy is the same. As we have now taken on the part of the father dog, we, too, should definitely insist that rules are adhered to.

Here is a concrete example. You take a small stick and use this 'prey' to offer a tug-of-war game to your dog. The little tot will go for it like greased lightning. He heartily bites into it and starts to 'fight' you for it. Just at this moment a butterfly flutters past, just in front of his nose. He takes this as an opportunity to break off the game with you, and clumsily chases after it. If you were to let him carry on now, you'd soon end up having a few relationship problems with your juvenile dog. So you continue with the play activity by inviting him once more to play with you. Now everything is back to where it should be, and you can then conclude the game whenever you want to.

One more time: the father dog would insist one hundred per cent on sticking to this rule – and as dog parent on two legs, so do we. Once this play-learning session has been concluded to your satisfaction, you can now have emotional social contact with the puppy, or, in other words, you may cuddle and canoodle him – preferably at nose level, so get yourself down on to the floor and get stuck in!

Now you have done everything correctly as far as your young charge, the puppy, is con-

You can vary the type of play with your dog as you please. Today we are playing a prey-cum-tug-of-war game. (Photo: Köppel)

cerned – and you have consolidated your relationship. As a reminder: tabooing, disciplining and play-based learning provide the foundations for this. Don't forget: playing with we humans and with other dogs is a decisive part of your dog's development.

If a puppy is not (sufficiently) allowed to play, this will inevitably lead to fundamental disturbances in the dog's psychological and emotional development. It is easy to understand that you cannot provide a good basis for a stress free development of his personality without play, even if this news hasn't yet permeated among all dog breeders, dog owners, or 'dog wrestlers'.

The fight game

In this game, tabooing and disciplining may seamlessly merge with each other. In order to get all three rolled into one, our dogs like to employ a fight game, because it contains all the elements that are needed for a social pack animal to become a fully fledged member of the dog pack and the human pack. In addition, using the fight game can effect a clear integration into the pack order and, by analogy, the integration into the human-dog pack, as well. Of course, these fight games don't involve real fighting in the sense of a fight to the death, where real damage would be done, such as may happen at some stage in the wild. No, such fight games serve to allow juvenile dogs to release the pent-up energy stemming from their ever increasing urge to be physically active, to practise their motor skills and to stabilise the pack order.

Let's now look a bit more closely at this fight game in order to filter out the essential aspects of our relationship work. Usually it begins without a 'proper' invitation to play (front legs wide apart, upper body bowed down). The dogs will lightly jump up against the other dog, but in a challenging manner, nudging or nipping each other's sides. This is followed by the attacker running off, as if taking flight. He will return straightaway in order to repeat the whole thing once more. At this point, at the latest, the invitation to play will be actively accepted by the 'victim'. Another variation of initiating a fight

Fight and scuffle games serve to maintain and nurture the pack order. (Photo: Köppel)

game consists of involving oneself in a prey game that is already underway. The holder of the prey will be 'attacked' following the same pattern as above. He will respond with a counterattack. Among dogs with healthy instincts, you will never see threatening or posturing behaviour involving real aggression during this sort of activity. What you will be able to see, however, is the complete spectrum of growling sounds and all kinds of biting. But as I said before, in these fight games they don't bite for real. There is, however, a small, but painful difference between humans and dogs; we haven't got any fur, and our delicate skin is considerably more vulnerable to the needle sharp little puppy teeth. Therefore we will have to point out to him that he has to be a tad more gentle with us. Here, too, you can use the species-appropriate disciplining technique described earlier.

A sub-type of the fight game is tapping, which was observed by H. Ludwig in the 1960s. Upon taking a closer look, it becomes obvious that this is not tapping in the actual sense, but rather the attempt to tread on the other dog's paws, a gesture that we now count among dominance and posturing behaviours. In practice, the tapping will look like this. Because each of the two dogs is trying to touch the opponent's paw first, an outsider might get the impression that both are continuously tapping each other in order to push the other dog away at the same time. In reality, neither dog wants to have his paws trodden on. On the other hand, they will both try to do exactly that to their opponent, again and again. This has the effect that in the majority of these attempts both will

collide in mid-air, and then rebound off each other in order to start another attack as quickly as possible. Because the motor skills of juvenile dogs are not yet fully developed, this often results in a loss of balance on both sides. This in turn provides a further incentive to grab the prey, followed by bite the prey, just as in the other fight game.

Any questions? Then off you go to start play-fighting with your dog! Assume the play position; with your legs wide apart and the upper body bowed down low, you start your first 'attack' on your canine friend's paws. You'll be surprised at his reaction! You'll also notice how quickly you can get him to lose his balance, and that's exactly what you'll do. In addition, continue to 'bite' him, with both hands and in various places.

Let's have another close look at 'biting', so we can incorporate it into our game to the maximum effect. The first thing we notice is that it is never done in the same spot for very long. So we don't grab our dog in only one spot, but – and it is best to use both hands for this – in several areas of his body at the same time. Grab his coat a few times, briefly and swiftly, and with varying degrees of vehemence, and you'll quickly be in your dog's good books, because he realises that you know how it's done!

You can refine this game by adding a further element: the paw-throat-neck grip. For this we grab our dog – as described above - with both hands, taking it in turns to grab him behind, at the front or at the side. It is important for this to always 'bite' the dog on his rear end with one of your hands. This way he has to defend himself against two 'attackers' at once.

Should our canine hothead get too worked up during this game, we'll quickly turn him on his back and demand his active submission. You should bear in mind that your dog ought to accept this unconditionally! While you are holding one hand on his throat he should remain still, and also display a 'smile', his head turned away from you. Slowly loosen your grip; he should keep lying down calmly. If he does this, everything is going well. If he tries to get away from you as soon as he can, and, on top of that, fidgets and fools about, tighten your grip again until he accepts it. Then he'll know that he is in safe hands with his (and for him this means in the proper sense) authoritarian pack boss. He

Every dog owner should carry out species-appropriate educational games, such as searching. (Photo: Köppel)

will now feel safe, and this, in turn has a positive effect on your relationship. The dog understands our rules and methods of upbringing with the goal of creating a bond of authority, because it relates to his ways and his language. In addition to furthering the bond with us, this experience also promotes his social competence regarding his environment, and he will never question your authority, even when he has grown up into a fine strapping dog.

Learning games

After the species-appropriate play-learning games, I'd like to present a few games that will increase our canine friend's cognitive abilities by an enormous amount. The following educational games should be viewed as suggestions only, and they can be designed individually. Give your imagination a free rein, and invent some games of your own.

Searching for a toy

This game is tailor-made to suit our dog's natural talents, and even when he is still only a puppy you can already lay the foundations for future tracking work. This works as follows. Take a toy that is suitable for a tug-of-war game. If you would like to do some tracking work with your dog at a later stage, use an old sock for this. Recall your dog and start the tug-of-war game with him. After a while, break this off and have your dog assume the 'sit' position. If your dog can't do 'sit' yet (which he really should be able to), you can get a second person to hold him. Walk away with the clearly visible toy, around the corner or to the nearest tree, and put it down, not particularly well hidden. Walk back to your dog, and with a 'search' despatch him in the direction of the hidden object. As this is easy to find this time round, he will quickly have discovered it. You will follow him in order to be able to start a tug-of-war game straightaway. By breaking off the game, you can immediately start a new search game. If you don't want to carry on playing any more, let the dog have the toy after the last search. Now he is allowed to play with it by himself. You can easily vary the search's level of difficulty. You can, for example, involve various rooms, several floors, and – as a final added detail – boxes, cupboards or similar things. It is important to have a tug-of-war game straight after the dog has found the object, in order to consolidate your relationship with the dog.

If you intend to do tracking work with your dog in the future, you should, as mentioned before, use an old sock instead of a toy. The sock will make an excellent search object when you begin doing tracking work. Also, you can make things easier by putting a bit of food inside the sock.

Variations of the search game

Take a bucket and a tug-of-war toy. Begin the game, then interrupt it, have your dog sit, and put the toy inside the bucket a few metres away, in an obvious manner. Go back and send your dog towards the bucket with the word for 'search'. Once he has arrived there and is eagerly looking around the bucket, possibly nudging it away, in order to get to his toy, start a tug-of-war game with him again.

Before using another variation of the search game, carry out a tug-of-war game with your dog. (Photo: Köppel)

Increase the level of difficulty by putting a second bucket next to the first, so that your dog is now faced with two possible places to look for the desired object. Once he has found it, have another tug-of-war game with him. You can increase the level of difficulty bit by bit by adding more buckets. The next step is to do the game without your dog being able to see you hiding his toy. This is one for specialists. For the last level, the one with multiple buckets, use more than one toy, so that he has to find several toys successfully before the tug-of-war game.

Searching for objects is fun, whether it's in snow or sand! (Photo: Köppel)

Searching in snow and sand

In the winter, if there is any snow, you can adapt the game described above as follows. Instead of the bucket, you use snow as a hiding place. Just bury the toy in the snow and make a little mound on top. Then despatch the dog on his search. The rest of the procedure is the same as described above. As an extension of the game you could make several snowy mounds, so that your dog has several search options. Finally, just as in the second game, the dog doesn't see where and how many toys you are hiding. A tip for a variation: instead of making the snow mounds close together in one row, spread them out over a larger area.

In the summer or in the absence of snow, you can play this game in sand. But take care that in his eagerness to find the toy your dog does not swallow any sand.

Searching up high

Our dog has now experienced the dimensions of length and width during his searches. In order to challenge him further we will now involve height, as well. This is easily incorporated into the first game. At home we can take a chest of drawers, a chair or a similar object of the same height, and put the toy on top. The procedure is otherwise identical with the search for toys. In order to enable him to find the toy quickly, we shouldn't make things too difficult for our dog at first. We slowly increase the level of difficulty. In addition we introduce a new word, such as 'high', for example, in order to be able to use it in difficult situations, such as during the free search in the great outdoors.

In order to expand the ability to master the new dimension of height further, we look for a forest that isn't too dense. For this game we need a ball that is suitable for a dog and made from a material that he won't be able to chew to pieces and swallow. We position ourselves at the edge of the forest and have our dog sit. We throw the ball as high as possible into the coppices of the trees, firstly, so that it is no longer a hundred percent visible for our dog, and secondly, so that it will constantly change direction as it is falling through the branches and twigs. As we throw the ball we say the word 'high', in order to clarify further the meaning of this new expression for our dog. In addition, the ball's changing direction during its fall promotes our dog's visual-motor skills. You can intensify this by going into denser forest, which will increase the level of difficulty.

The Training of perception and reflexes

The following game promotes the dog's visual perception and reflexes. For this you need, for example, a stone wall with an uneven surface. Position yourself a few metres away from the wall and throw the ball at the wall. The ball will bounce off in various unpredictable angles. This will stretch dog's visual skills considerably, and at the same time he will be excited, because he has to react spontaneously to the ball's trajectory.

If you don't have a suitable wall at your disposal, you'll be able to achieve the same with a rubber ball that is square instead of round, because it will bounce off in an unpredictable direction.

Developing strategies

If your dog enjoys water and swimming, and you know a small water source or a waterfall, you have the following opportunity for a game: throw the ball directly into the jet of water, so that it will be kept in one place by it, then send your dog to fetch the ball. He will have to develop his own strategy to work out the best way to extract it. In addition, this provides a welcome way to cool down in the summer!

In order to get to the ball, the dog has to find a solution by himself. (Photo: Köppel)

Communal games

You and your dog can do the following two games on your own. However, playing them together with other dogs hugely increases their attraction.

Searching together

Have the dogs sit, preferably in a row, so they have equal chances at the starting point. If there is an older dog among them, give him a handicap. Now one of the humans hides, or alternatively a toy is hidden. Upon calling a word such as 'search', the dogs are allowed to search for the human or the toy together. The dog who has found the toy may keep it as an object of prestige, and he can – if the group dynamics are thus inclined – begin a game of running and hunting for the prey with it. If a human was the object of the search, he can have a ball, a ring or something of the sort on him, and use it to initiate a hunt for the prey after being discovered.

Walking together

Have your dogs sit on the start line in the same way as for the searching together game. After that, the dog owners walk away. Here you can choose between the variations of sprint and long distance. No matter which one you decided to go for, following a signal all dog owners simultaneously give permission for their dogs to start running. Whoever reaches their mistress or master first is allowed to have a boisterous playing session with them. This way, everybody wins; this is very Olympic, because all that matters is the taking part!

A final word about putting species-appropriate play between human and dog into practice. Of course, everybody has their individual ways that come out when they're playing with their dog. That's why you shouldn't put yourself under any pressure, if you are experiencing difficulties with any of this. What is much more important is that you recognise and internalise the principle of species-appropriate play in your dog's upbringing. If this is the case, you can proceed following your own personal preference and ability. Just put yourself in your dog's shoes, and he will reward you for it with a harmonious and problem-free friendship. However, you must never forget one thing: even if our way of playing is as species-appropriate as possible, for our dog it will never really be quite the same as playing with his canine pals. That's why, particularly in his youth, you should always offer him sufficient space and time to play with his own kind!

The next question is: when can you really start to let rip properly while playing with your dog? The 'golden rule' says after one year. But how would this be dealt with in the wild? Do dogs living in the wild stick to this golden rule as well?

As we know, the mother dog looks after the puppies exclusively until their eighth week of life. After that, the other legal guardian, usually the biological father, takes over. While the puppies were restricted in their physical activities to the immediate environment of their cave, i.e., their camp, up to this point, now there is a drastic change. The mother dog suddenly invites the male, who was up to now a complete nonentity in her eyes, to engage in a game with her. He is quite incredulous, but seizes his chance, and instantly gets involved in a running game with her. Both scamper about boisterously as if they were still teenagers themselves. This sudden turn-up for the books does not escape the puppies' attention, and they come running, full of curiosity. They are very astonished by what they see, because first of all, mum is playing not with them, but with someone else, and secondly, the two of them are running further and further away from the cave! The children simply have to scuttle after them, because safety, as they know it, is only with mum. The two 'lovebirds' happily carry on running and play-

The dog, who is a runner by nature, needs to be able to run to be healthy. And off we go! (Photo: Köppel)

ing, with the band of kids following in their wake throughout. Not exactly a marathon, but comparable to a ten to fifteen-minute walk. In addition, this is cross-country terrain, where the occasional little incline has to be scaled. By way of this ritual play, the father now takes over his children's upbringing. In the period that follows he moves further and further away from the camp, steadily increasing the distance – and with good reason! He knows that in three months' time his kids, at the age of five months, will have to join the hunt as juvenile dogs. This can easily involve thirty to eighty kilometres of running per day! In order to learn how to hunt, the young dogs have to watch the older dogs, and this is only possible if they can keep up.

So much about the golden rule. I don't mean by this that you should take your four-month-old dog on a marathon. Exercising him, yes, but not in an exaggerated way that would overtax him. As an observant dog owner you will quickly realise when your dog has reached his limits. Doing this you will also notice that, contrary to popular opinion, these are able to be stretched by a surprising amount. But let's have another look at the exercise programme that the father dog undertakes with his puppies. From about the tenth week onwards, he continuously leads his charges towards ever more new playgrounds, each further away from the camp than the previous one. If playground number one was an almost level piece of meadow, playground number two will offer quite a sharp increase in difficulty. Here you will find more or less lumpy terrain with steep little slopes, the whole thing overgrown with thick bushes and undergrowth. The slopes are good for exercising co-ordination and strength, because if you don't pay attention, you'll tumble down and have to start from the bottom again, or you may trip in the bushes and undergrowth and get stuck. Then it's full steam ahead or wriggling out backwards. At the end you'll gallop up a steep hill together, happy to be hugged by the father dog as a reward. This way the challenges are increased every time, and the little whippersnappers become more and more skilled and co-ordinated.

You begin to get an idea, where I'm heading to. Exactly: to a question whose inevitability is due to some hard-to-kill myths: from what age onwards should my puppy be allowed to climb stairs? The answer, biologically speaking, is from the eighth week onwards, as long as the stairs have a normal gradient and aren't in excess of ten storeys high. A puppy should actually climb stairs with ten to fifteen steps several times every day in order to exercise and train his co-ordination and his musculoskeletal system. Of course, this should never be overdone while the dog is still growing. Under no circumstances should you mollycoddle your puppy until he has reached the age of eight months or even more, and then train him with the short, sharp shock method. This would inevitably lead to greater potential damage than strengthening the puppy's musculoskeletal system steadily and continuously. Why don't we just do it the same way as the father dog?

Dogs are runners after all, and if we keep this in mind, we know what we owe to our dog: exercise that is adapted to the dog's age. A dog owner who does not walk seven uninterrupted kilometres with their juvenile dog should give the matter some thought, always provided that the juvenile dog is healthy and not overweight. As this leads us to a further important issue, we'll take another look at our wild dog pack, in order to see how they deal with nutrition.

After the exclusive bond between mother and puppies is severed, the absolute priority with regard to feeding that the puppies have enjoyed over the adult dogs also comes to an end. Sensibly this happens during the socialisation phase, because at the same time the baby dog, who is perhaps still under the impression that he is the centre of the world, is supposed to become a social pack animal. The adult dogs still have the task of feeding the entire pack, including the young, but this is becoming increasingly difficult because the nutritional needs of the youngsters are steadily increasing as they grow. The effort of hunting, and with it the energy needs of the adult dogs, rises to a considerable level. Hence they need and claim the lion's share of the prey for themselves. The juveniles have to contend themselves with what's left. This has nothing to do with antisocial behaviour. On the contrary, if an adult dog was to starve, the impact this would have on the entire pack would be dramatic, because it is the adult dogs who are able to lead a pack and ensure its survival in the most trying of circumstances. This is something the young dogs have yet to learn. In contrast, the loss of a juvenile dog can be compensated for without affecting the whole pack system.

The feeding rights of the puppies undergo a rapid change during this period. Their turn comes only when the adult dogs have had their fill. It is only natural that the best pieces should be eaten by the parents – at this time they need the most nutritious food available! And what does our own pack's nutrition plan look like? Usually the complete contrary to how it's done in the wild. The puppy and juvenile dog get special 'premium food' possibly even a very special 'pedigree food'. Upon looking more closely at the contents of this 'special' food, you'll discover that their usefulness regarding a species-appropriate feeding plan is more than questionable. If on top of this the dog is being overfed due to misplaced love, we've got a problem! The dog will become lazy as a result, and this is how you end up in a vicious circle. Shouldn't it be enough that we humans are constantly forced to battle against obesity? Do we really have to infect our best friend with this plague as well?

Let your juvenile dog play with other dogs as often as possible. (Photo: Köppel)

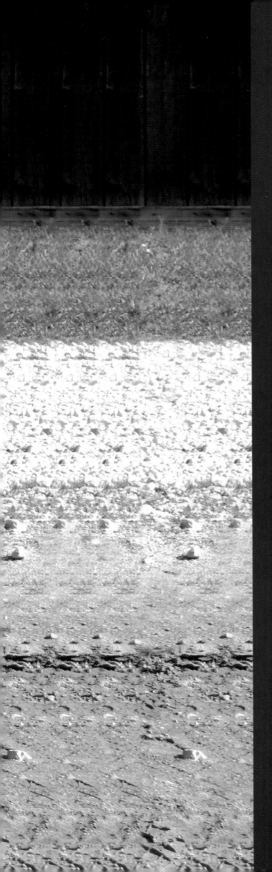

Basic training: the concentration exercise
'sit'

The concentration exercise 'sit' represents the basis of the relationship training with your dog. It can be used at any age, whether you are starting to bring up a puppy, or if you are undertaking a 'changing of the pack' with an older dog. This basic training contains all the elements that are needed for species-appropriate upbringing.

The basic exercise 'sit' is an important concentration exercise. (Photo: Köppel)

The meaning of the exercise

You may perhaps ask yourself why I am calling it the concentration exercise 'sit'. Let's look at it from a behaviourist perspective. In the first two to three weeks of life, the mother dog is lying next to her puppies to suckle them. From the third week onwards she will stand up so the puppies can suckle from her teats while sitting down. While doing so, they are pawing the mother's teats in order to stimulate the flow of milk. This, by the way, explains the 'handshake' that can be observed among adult dogs, as well. It is therefore not meant as a gesture of appeasement, but as begging the superior dog's favour.

For the puppies, the act of sitting down is first of all something to do with feeding or food, For this reason it is relatively simple to teach a dog to 'sit'. You only have to provoke your dog to get into a food expectation mode by, for example, holding a treat in your closed hand, and he will instantly sit down in front of you. Another thing can be observed: once the dog gets the food – or not, as the case may be – he immediately gets up again! This is based on the simple fact that the expectation of food has either been satisfied or not, which dissolves the associated neuronal tension, i.e., concentration. Every time your dog enters a mode of expectation this will enhance his concentration, and we're going to take advantage of exactly this behaviour for our concentration exercise 'sit'.

Execution

- Assume a squatting position. To him this is the body language signal for coming to you.

- Don't remain in this position until he has reached you, but get up again once your dog is about a metre away from you, This is a form of authority based on body language, and your dog will stop and possibly even sit down already, without you having said anything.

- If he just stands there, ask him to 'sit'. (If he runs straight past you, however, he is making a clear statement about what he really thinks of you: you are definitely a good playmate and fur-stroker, as well as one of the best tin-openers in the world, but, alas, not a pack leader!)
- Take a few paces backwards, immediately after the dog has sat down.

- Whatever you do, don't turn around, because this would be the body language signal for your dog to follow you.
- Stop there for a little while, thus initiating the concentration phase. During this, in spite of not getting any food or any other form of attention, the dog should stay sitting down and instead of concentrating on the anticipated food, he should concentrate on you, his boss.

- For most dogs this in itself is difficult enough. If he manages it, we have achieved a significant step in his education. If your dog has been concentrating on you and has remained sitting there, tell him that he has done well by playing a game with him. Slowly walk up to your dog once more, and stop a short distance away from him.

- Use one particular word that is only used for releasing the dog from the concentration phase, and start a tug-of-war game with him. Give your dog a proper run for his money, back and forth, and once in a while let him pull you in his direction as well.

This means that it is not only up to you to determine the direction of the game, but that your dog also has a say in it.

- Break off the game by saying 'Let go'. Don't look at your dog while doing this, but instead make a conscious effort to look the other way and move away from him.
- If your dog accepts this immediately by letting go, move further away from him and keep changing direction. This enables you to see whether your dog is following you, or

whether he is busy engaging in other activities, such as sniffing or running off.

- If he runs off or sniffs around, recall him immediately and initiate a new concentration phase. This doesn't have to be for very long.

- If the dog accepts your offer to stop playing, and follow you instead, you have already reached a milestone in your species appropriate relationship.
- If the procedure has been consolidated up to this point, you can turn round towards your dog again, in order to have another concentration exercise straight afterwards.
- There are further details and modules regarding the concentration exercise 'sit' in my book 'The Pack Concept'.

You are just giving him the opportunity to show you once again that he wants to play with you. Please keep in mind that the father dog, the pack boss, is the one who determines the time, object and duration of play.

Using the
method of the
pack concept
for tracking
training

As mentioned before, we should use our dog's budding urge to expand his territory for tracking work during the pack order phase at the latest. This promotes his intellectual faculties and strengthens the 'team spirit' of our relationship. I would like to introduce you to tracking training according to the pack concept, building on the foundations that you have achieved already.

Step by step towards the object of the search

For this you'll need:

- a leash, about two to three metres long
- old discarded socks
- a collar

The use of a tracking harness is optional. Experience has shown, however, that the following method leads to better results, especially with search novices.

- Begin a tug-of-war game with your dog using one of the socks.

- Interrupt play and have your dog assume the 'sit' position.

- Attach the leash to the collar and put it between the dog's front legs.

- Walk a few metres backwards and recall your dog, the leash trailing between his legs.

- Have him assume the 'sit' position once more, and walk away backwards while you show your dog the sock in your hands, using it to motivate him.

- Walk back the same way you came straight away.

- The level of the motivating action has to be adapted to the dog's character. He should not be motivated so strongly as to make him want to dash towards you straightaway, but only as far as is needed to increase his level of attention.

- After five minutes, stop and throw the sock in front of you.

- Just before you have reached your dog, turn back towards the track, while saying 'Search'. Once the dog starts running, pick up the leash directly behind him and walk or run after him towards the search object. Most dogs will make an enthusiastic dash for the track, in order to get to the toy. You can simply follow behind.

- Just before your dog has reached the object, say 'Down' to him, this way he'll learn to 'point' to the search objects, as it is known in dog trainer jargon, at the same time.

- We want to preserve his motivation and his enthusiasm. That's why at this stage it doesn't matter whether your dog uses his nose or his eyes for the search. We'll leave that up to him for now. At this point the shared enjoyment of the 'team search' is the sole objective.

- If this has gone according to plan, take the leash off the dog, who is still lying in the 'down' position, and begin a tug-of- war game with him.

- At the end of the game, let him have the 'trophy' and have a bit of a tussle with him.

Some dogs that are already fixated on treats may evade the motivation game, because their relationship with their human isn't quite sorted yet. In this case, you take the sock and put some food inside.

- Proceed the same way as described above, with the difference that you let your dog sniff the sock while he is sitting in front of you. But only that: under no circumstances must he be allowed to eat the food out of the sock!
- After that proceed as described above.

This method should only be used in an extreme emergency, and even then only as briefly as possible. Letting the dog sniff the food should be replaced by play as soon as possible.

Increasing the search distance

Once the first part of the tracking training works well, you should move on. The next step is to increase the search distance, again tailoring it to suit the individual temperament of the dog.

- If your dog was successful at five metres, slowly increase the distance to ten metres.
- If you were able to conduct a search of a distance of ten metres before, increase it to twenty metres.
- In addition, we lay the track across a very varied terrain. This can cause irritation at first, which in turn can lead to mistakes in the search for the track. We will not correct the mistakes straightaway, but let him try and find the track again on his own at first. This promotes his self-reliance and his cognitive abilities. To have the dog learning from his mistakes will lead to a better result, rather than correcting the dog immediately every time.
- Once this lesson works well, proceed to the next stage. For this, we increase the distance between us and the dog on the leash bit by bit. The exam guidelines for the tracking exam stipulates that the search leash has to be ten metres long. Once the dog is searching confidently on a long leash, we are ready for the next step.
- Now we begin to build the first change of direction into the tracking route.
- Lay a track in the same way as explained before.
- At the point where you have put down the final object, just step a metre sideways. You

don't actually turn off to one side at ninety degrees, but you really take two to three sideways steps.

- Afterwards you walk six to seven metres further backwards and put down the final object.

- Retrace your exact steps to the beginning and start the search with your dog. It is important to move slowly along the search leash towards your dog, as soon as you approach change in direction, so you can initially give him extra support for the additional challenge.
- Allow your dog to search without correcting him, even if he doesn't follow the exact track.
- Some dogs just run to the final search object via the shortest possible route. In this case, have the dog sit at the starting position for a while, before starting the search. The prolonged concentration phase will make your dog search in a markedly calmer and more concentrated manner.
- As soon as possible, adapted to the dog's learning process, try to replace the sideways section of the route by a section that has been walked in a forward direction.

Having fun as a team

Once this training unit regarding the track search has been completed to everyone's satisfaction, you have basically achieved the foundations for a track exam. After that, the incorporation of further changes of direction, as well as an increased distance of the search route are only a matter of practice.

The idea behind the tracking training according to the pack concept method is not purely about the training of tracking dogs, but rather about building trust and enhancing the team spirit. Your dog is being challenged from the onset to think for himself, because he is not distracted from the real subject, the independent search for treats.

The enjoyment offered by joint activities should always be the main objective. If you want to pass an exam, having developed a certain ambition in this area, do go ahead! But always remember that all that counts is taking part!

If you are among those who want to do this work 'only' for themselves and with the aim of improving their relationship with their dog, then you can happily modify the tracking training now and then. You can decide how your dog should to the pointing. He can do this in the 'down', the 'sit' or the 'stand' position, but it is also possible to use the version where your dog fetches the object to you. Just use your imagination...

Feeding
your dog
sensibly

Of course, every responsible dog owner only wants the best for this dog, and hence there are many myths, semi-scientific truths and wild speculations surrounding the subject of nutrition. The various offers of dog food stand out just as prominently as the offers of educational and training methods for dogs, as well as the ideas disseminated by the proponents of the different viewpoints regarding the correct nutrition for dogs.

Strictly speaking the dog is not a carnivore, but rather an eater of whole animals. (Photo: Brodmann)

Dry, raw or boiled?

For some, dry dog food is the only real food for the dog, while others denounce it, advocating moist food instead, i.e., tinned food with flakes. Other 'experts' and dog owners think that only raw butcher's scraps, or something similar, make a suitable food for dogs. The latter feeding option is experiencing a new boom in the dog scene at the moment, bearing the ominous name BARF. Apparently BARF is an acronym for Biologically Appropriate Raw Food, and is gaining popularity in the dog world.

The central idea behind it is to feed the dog natural, unprocessed food: fresh meat with vegetables, if possible without chemical additives. Vegetables of any kind – whether they are raw or boiled – are nutritionally useless for the dog, because he lacks the necessary enzymes to digest them, a fact that is conveniently forgotten by the promoters of BARF. For a dog, vegetables consist of nothing but fibre and they have no nutritional value for him at all. This is something those advocating the feeding of carrots, which is still being preached by some, should take note of as well. Some authors are prescribing the feeding of raw sliced carrots, others advise boiling and puréeing them before feeding them to the dog.

When using the BARF method, the first question the dog owner is confronted with is: how do I avoid feeding either excessive or insufficient amounts of the required vital substances such as proteins, fats and vitamins. Butcher's scraps may also contain harmful substances, and fresh meat from the butcher can be very expensive in the long run. Further research would probably reveal that meat has to be bled dry before leaving the abattoir. In nutritional terms this represents a real deficiency, because blood contains essential minerals and salts that the dog urgently requires to stay healthy. Apart from this, all the suitable raw materials for feeding a dog are either deficient in calcium and/or are too rich in phosphorous and/or they are deficient in vitamins, particularly vitamin A.

Finally, as it turns out, there is no shortage of literature on the subject either, although this seems to be full of contradicting opinions regarding the individual ingredients that should be contained in the food, and in what quantities. Not surprisingly, in the end you are left none the wiser. Of course, there will always be those who just have a natural talent for such things and who can feed their dog healthy food without any scientific recipes, just as there are people who are green-fingered, and who manage to get any plant entrusted to their care to flower and thrive. But as the 'only true' nutritional concept, BARF will most probably not make a suitable dog food for the population of dog owners at large.

A dog needs more than meat

After all that, what is the healthiest option for your dog? In order to answer this better, let us take a look at his gastro-intestinal and nutritional physiology. Scientifically speaking, the dog is classified as a meat eater, a carnivore.

From a biological perspective, however, this is incorrect because in the wild dogs don't just eat meat, but also mushrooms, fruit and – importantly – predigested vegetable matter from their prey's digestive tracts. No wolf or dog would be able to survive on meat alone, if by meat you mean mainly the prey's muscle fibre. Even if you were to add various edible giblets into the term 'meat', you'd still end up with a deficient diet. Even pronounced carnivores, such as cats, are unable to live off meat as their sole diet in the long term. In the wild, even large prey, such as buffalo or deer is eaten whole. It would therefore be much more precise to talk about the dog as a 'whole animal eater', or 'faunivore', scientifically speaking. There is nothing more difficult, however, than to expunge a popularly applied term, no matter how erroneous it may be, from people's minds and from literature alike. Exactly the same applies to the term 'omnivore'.

Pigs and humans can be counted among these, but dogs most certainly cannot. But it is not even one hundred per cent true of pigs and humans, because no human or pig will eat 'everything'. What is meant by this definition is merely the fact that these species need animal as well as vegetable-based diets. In order to stay healthy, the omnivore needs a balanced variety of food stuffs tailored to his requirements, as is the case with every other species. This is exactly what a wolf or dog's kill will provide to perfection, ranging from the different meats of varying quality to the predigested plant mash in its intestines.

The correct food

No matter how beautiful and natural it may seem, we cannot provide a proper diet to our dog by feeding him a purely on raw ingredients. With a view to a balanced diet, tinned dog food offers more disadvantages than advantages. Despite being promoted by the dog food industry as the 'freshest' way of feeding your dog, upon taking a closer look, the contrary seems to be the case. This is mainly due to the 'moisture content', meaning nothing other than water. To prevent this 'moisture content' from going off, genuine preserved food has to be heated to high temperatures for prolonged periods of time. After this most of the 'freshness' will have evaporated. In addition, synthetic preservatives and moisturising agents are added to 'maintain quality', which cannot possibly be in the interest of a species-appropriate and natural diet for a dog. Regarding value for money, tinned dog food also leaves a lot to be desired. Because of the high water content of twenty to thirty per cent, the energy density is far lower than with alternative food types; you need a lot more to get the same result.

Nor should one forget that all the tins and trays that provide the packaging for the moist food have to be disposed of as well.

Last but not least, this leaves the option of dried food, which from my perspective I can unreservedly recommend. During the production of dried food, great care is taken not only to ensure the use of high-quality protein, but also regarding the correct vitamin and mineral content, as well as the all-important trace elements. Added enzymes ensure that the dog can utilise the vegetable content of the food, and the particular way of preparing the food ensures that the nutritional content is distributed evenly throughout. The choice of dried foods on offer is almost overwhelming, so as the consumer, you have to be well-informed. The really good products are actually in the minority. Often the smaller local dried food manufacturers can be recommended most of all.

Now you just have to hope that your dog (and therefore you) is not afflicted by the modern plague of food allergies, because this means that the breeder from whom you bought the dog has done something wrong. Why, you can read in the next chapter…

For dog breeders
and those wanting to become dog breeders...

This chapter is particularly close to my heart. This is because whether we get to have the dogs who are healthy or dogs who are sick, who are behaviourally affected or normal, is in the hands of the dog breeders. Dodgy breeders do great business out of inexperienced customers and those who won't take the time to think about things properly.

The breeders carry a special responsibility.
(Photo: Köppel)

These breeders have no problems switching from one breed, which they were once sworn to, to another, because the former may not be as profitable any more due to new animal protection legislation, such as, for example, the docking ban. Or they switch to another pedigree breed that has just become the latest fad and is therefore particularly lucrative at the moment; the demand determines the supply!

If a pedigree breed has a high stock market value, it will increasingly be bred. Nobody seems to be bothered, at least not at the point of buying the dog, by the fact that quantity doesn't necessarily equal quality. Only a few months later, the dog owners wake up to the fact that the fantastic champion right at the top of the line didn't just pass his beauty on to his offspring, but also a whole array of illnesses. The impressively colourful papers called the family tree won't be much good now. With the horrendous vet bills comes the great disillusionment, and many a dog from such a 'pedigree breeder' will end up in a dogs' home – or even worse, tied to the nearest lamp post or parking sign and abandoned.

If the breeder is a member of a breed club, there are various conditions that he has to fulfil, if he wants to climb up the dog breeder's ladder of success. As with many things in the dog scene, everything is taken into account, except one thing: the dog. Almost every breed club has different breeding regulations and guidelines, which are usually not primarily concerned with the dog's health, but rather with the breeder's prestige and financial well-being.

Real dog-lovers want dogs who are healthy in mind and body, who will accompany us throughout their dog life (which is far too short as it is) with a maximum of joy and happiness! For this we need good breeders who are real dog-lovers – and fortunately they still exist. It is easy to establish a solid basis for any kind of breeding, if you take the following recommendations on board. These were developed by Professor Georg Wilhelm Rieck as early as the 1960s. Even then, he foresaw the direction in which the development of pedigree dog breeding was heading. These recommendations were presented to the world of dog breeding at an international congress in the 1970s, and to this day have not received a great deal of a response. I wonder why.

The most important recommendations for the breeding of pedigree dogs

Strict selection by the breeder

The highest maxim in the battle against genetic defects is the strict exclusion from further breeding of litters who contain malformed puppies, as well as the rigorous exclusion of negative heterozygotic parents. At the risk of sounding a little grandiose, I'll have to use a few scientific terms for this. Dog genetics are based on genetic polymorphism. Polymorphism means that there are several different versions of a gene (alleles) that have the relevant characteristics. The more developed the genetic polymorphism is in a population, i.e., a comprehensive group of individuals, the better their ability to adapt to changing environmental conditions will be.

Breeding is a complicated matter that could, however, be simplified, if the most important recommendations were heeded. (Photos: Köppel)

This is also called passing on heterozygotic genes. Heterozygotic simply means hybrid. Dogs possess homologous chromosomes that are occupied by two different alleles, i.e., two different versions of the same gene. The mode of inheritance – dominance-recessivity, codominance, incomplete dominance – decides which allele is dominant. If two individuals with a defective genetic make-up mate, i.e., the male and the female dog, the result are malformations and diseases. This also means that it would not make any sense to mate a female dog who is carrying defective genetic material with a male dog who is entirely unconnected to the female line. Even if the male does not possess the defective genes that would make the genetic defect become apparent, their descendants would nevertheless carry the mother's genes, which in turn they will pass on to their offspring and thus on to the population at large. The same applies to a male dog with defective genes.

If dogs who are carriers of defective genetic material were not excluded from breeding, the result would be that in the long run hidden defective genes would inevitably accumulate in that particular pedigree breeding pool; and they can manifest themselves uncontrollably at any time and in any litter.

Honest reporting by breeders

If you remind yourself of the first recommendation, you will realise that really successful breeding can only be ensured in the long run if the breed clubs report about their activities truthfully and in good faith. This means the painstaking reporting of every single puppy with a birth defect.

Searching for the causes

Likewise, all still-born puppies or those who died immediately after birth have to be handed over to the respective breed warden or to the vet for an autopsy. This is the only way to ensure that research into the causes and work towards the limitation of genetic diseases will be possible in the future.

The nonsense of limiting litter sizes

At the extreme end of the spectrum there is the notion that the number of puppies per litter that are raised into adulthood should be limited. Genetically speaking, this would only serve to obscure the true state of affairs. It is quite possible that a bitch who possesses formidable instincts will raise ten or in exceptional cases even more puppies without any human assistance. It would be a great pity if such a bitch were to be excluded from the breeding process. In contrast, a bitch who is unable to raise four or five puppies on her own would have a negative impact on the biologically sound breeding of dogs. For today's breeding purposes I would suggest an average number of eight puppies as an ideal litter size. There must be no human intervention in raising the puppies.

Continuous training for breed wardens

Because Mendel, with his easily understandable laws of heredity, is no longer able to help to us regarding the origins of the complex interaction at the root of genetic diseases, the breed clubs, or rather their umbrella organisation, should make sure that the breed warden's training in the field of polymorphous population genetics is continuously brought up to date. The whole

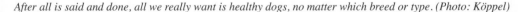

After all is said and done, all we really want is healthy dogs, no matter which breed or type. (Photo: Köppel)

thing sounds more difficult than it is, and it is also possible to put complex scientific findings in clearly structured words. This, however, would require the umbrella organisation, as well as the clubs themselves, to take matters in hand.

Incestuous mating for test purposes

At first you will probably be surprised by this recommendation. The most important and, at the same time, most simple way of developing a biologically sound dog breeding business is the use of incestuous mating. This simple breeding method enables you to sort out healthy genetic material from defective genetic material very quickly and effectively. Because closely related individuals, i.e., father, mother, daughter, son, have almost identical genes, the alleles, the different versions of a gene are situated in the same location on the chromosome. An individual with a two-fold set of chromosomes can never have more than two genes that are related to each other via these alleles.

The parent animal passes only one allele on to its offspring. Any already obvious, as well as recessively dormant, hereditary defects that are present will now manifest themselves.

Every club should use incestuous mating to begin with in order to establish which dogs are suitable for a sound breeding operation. If a mother dog is mated with one of her sons, and the result is a litter of healthy puppies, the breeder can be sure that he can register the mother with the club's breeding pool. The same goes for the father dog, should he also live with the breeder. In due course, this will lead to an ever increasing breeding pool of biologically sound dogs, whose genetic status should be checked by incestuous test matings at regular intervals. Of course, this is not about promoting permanent incestuous mating, but rather about recognising genetically pathogenic dogs and thereby defective genetic material in order to eliminate them from the breeding process. In the 1960s and 1970s the Hoechst corporation came up with successful examples for this strategy, and my friend and mentor Eberhard Trumler also employed it with good results over several generations during his breeding research programmes

Rethinking the selection criteria

Every breed club has based its breeding criteria first and foremost on breed characteristics, such as body shape and colour, which are randomly labelled as 'beautiful'. These rather old-fashioned criteria should urgently be looked at again from a biological point of view, and corrected.

I'll just mention two examples, because any more would exceed the remit of this book. During the breeding experiments I already mentioned, the Hoechst corporation, as well as Eberhard Trumler, discovered a very important biological marker: the amount of pigment on the dog's skin. It is very easy to see whether a dog has good or bad pigmentation levels. The pads, claws, lips and nose should be dark, even in dogs with white fur. The fur colour has nothing to do with pigmentation, but the dog's skin should not be pink. Dogs who don't fulfil these criteria usually have pathogenic genes. We know from human and veterinary medical science that a lack of pigmentation can be associated with various metabolic disorders, which in the absence of biologically controlled breed-

We should urgently say goodbye to outdated and erroneous opinions, as well as mediaeval teachings about dog breeding. (Photo: Brodmann)

Looking at the dog's brain anatomy, we can see that the social motors of dog behaviour are situated in the frontal parts of the cerebrum, the frontal lobes. If the skull is manipulated by the use of breeding techniques to achieve 'breed specific standards', as is the case with the bull terrier's 'downface', this has an effect on the brain housed below. Brain performance can be reduced, or the dog's social behaviour can be affected. Selective breeding doesn't just allow you to determine the fur colour and build, but also the brain volume. All those who are breeding dogs with extreme skull shapes should think about this very carefully!

No obscuring of genetic defects

Under no circumstance must dogs selected for the breeding pool be subjected to surgical intervention in order to obscure genetic defects, such as, for example, the relatively common cryptoorchism, which usually causes the testicles to remain inside the abdomen. Such operations should only be carried out on dogs who don't have a breeding certificate.

Reviewing breeders' decrees

When amendments are made to the breeding regulations, all breeding clubs should act on them. The breeders' decrees should be reviewed, and breed wardens, as well as breeders should receive intensive training in this regard. For the clubs, this means a great investment of time and money. In order to secure this project financially, perhaps a small breeding fee could be raised by every club. Alternatively, the clubs and associations could establish a central funding body.

ing can have detrimental effects on the entire population. Therefore it is vital to have a selection based on the amount of skin pigmentation.

For the second example I will quote the afore – mentioned Professor Rieck, who is the author of the ten recommendations in this chapter: 'The requirements needed to fulfil the "standard" can lead to a reduction of the circumference of certain organs, as is the case with one particular breed that is required to have a "a skull that is flat and not domed, which has no noticeable end".' This will most certainly be resulting in a reduction of brain volume – with all its consequences for these animals' intelligence – and promoting diseases of a cerebral nature and potential behavioural disturbances.

Putting the biological breeding approach into practice

I don't have any illusions about the feedback I'll be getting regarding this biological breeding approach. Among the breeding community there are after all people who pursue very simple goals with their breeding operations: money, prestige, etc. But I'll keep the inextinguishable flame of hope alive inside me that there may be enough breeders who follow alternative beliefs, and who are interested in healthy dogs for the future. Then we would not have any cause to worry about our wonderful pedigree dog breeds!

I don't want to conclude this chapter about dog breeding without pointing to another deplorable state of affairs that is spreading steadily. I'm talking about allergies, such as food allergies. The causes are easily uncovered. Once again, breeding is at the root of this evil. When the outward appearance is held far above the biological being, i.e., health, there will be more and more dogs with genetic defects. In truth, it would be very simple to avert this development by only using dogs with good pigmentation for breeding – because, as mentioned above, good pigmentation is a sign of a sound state of health. Medically, this can be explained as follows. In the early embryonic stage the brain, the nervous system and the skin, including the mucus membranes are situated in the same cotyledon. If, during further developmental stages, a lack of pigmentation is noticeable from the outside, then that is the proof that there is a genetic error in this area, which means a predisposition for allergies and other, atopic reactions without predisposition to any particular type of allergy.

The second point is that the modern disinfection frenzy has now reached many breeders. Visitors are only allowed to see the puppies from the fifth week onwards, because breeders assume that the puppies' immune system is not sufficiently developed before that. Visitors are forced to pass through the breeder's 'disinfection lock'. As we know clearly from human and veterinary medical research and experience, our immune system – and that of the dog – needs a certain amount of bacteria or viruses, in order to be able to develop the necessary immune responses. Only after this 'training' can the organism defend itself against any kind of germs. An immune system that has not been allowed to do this will (due to a complete lack of 'coolness') develop a tendency to overreact with fits of 'hysteria' to completely harmless proteins in the food, mistaking them for hostile substances, and what you end up with is the perfect allergy.

(Photo: Köppel)

Popular misconceptions and a new approach to **understanding dogs**

As this book is reaching its final stages I feel I must deal with a few popular misconceptions that are persistently making the rounds in the dog scene. In addition, I'd like to explain a few everyday dog behaviours that are known to every dog owner, in slightly more depth. You will be astonished – and possibly view your dog with different eyes afterwards!

A dog who is in an elevated position is not going to doubt your authority as a result. (Photo: Köppel)

Gestures of appeasement and their meaning

First of all there are the calming signals, the gestures of appeasement that are all based on incorrect interpretations. I would like to look closer at the most popular of these, the yawn. It has been interpreted as an appeasement gesture, even though from a behavioural point of view it is the external sign of a bipolar thought process, a thought process that has two different intentions colliding with each other. The tension caused by these conflicting intentions is resolved by the dog yawning, and this is visible to those around him as well. An example: you have played with your dog; because you have other things to do, you say 'Let go' to your dog in order to take the toy out of your dog's mouth, thus ending the game. Your dog would like to carry on playing. He is not quite sure what to do. Having accepted the 'let go', he tries to persuade you to start playing once more by jumping up at you. You emphatically prevent him from doing this. Your dog remains standing and starts to yawn. By doing so he resolves the inner conflict between him wanting to carry on playing, while the boss says the game is over. Yawning does not mean appeasement, but it always means that in this particular situation the dog would rather like to do something else than he actually ends up doing, usually not quite voluntarily. If you observe your dog closely for a while you will be amazed to realise that this interpretation explains a lot of situations rather well. You don't have to yawn together with your dog any more in order to appease him, because from a behaviourist point of view this is plain nonsense!

Many popular misconceptions, such as the calming signal, cause misunderstandings rather than a species-appropriate harmonious relationship. (Photo: Köppel)

The meaning of the elevated position

Another popular misconception is the notion that the dog must not be 'above' us, and this is meant in a literal sense! Some people who are, or aspire to be, dog trainers and dog psychologists believe in all seriousness that the dog must not be allowed to be lying on the first floor while you are on the ground floor. This way the dog would be dominant, because he is 'above' his boss. This story should be confined to the realm of dog myths, along with many others. It is sufficient to watch a wild dog pack to realise this: the pack leaders aren't bothered by other pack members, including older puppies or juveniles, lying at a higher level to them – nature usually isn't flat as a pancake either – because this does not diminish their authority in any way. You, who have a good relationship with your dog, can leave him lying on the floor above, if that's what he wants – he would probably rather be near you anyway.

Who walks through the door first?

The same sort of misunderstanding is at the root of the belief that the human, i.e., the dog owner, should always be the first to walk through doors or any narrow passages in order to show his dog who's boss. From a behaviourist point of view, this is complete nonsense. If pack leaders always had to walk ahead, in certain situations this could have quite negative consequences for the entire pack.

Let's imagine the following scene. The pack is out hunting. The dogs have separated their weakened prey from the rest of the herd and have increased its state of panic further by a number of simulated attacks. The hunted animal tries anything to escape from this situation. It mobilises his last bit of strength and escapes to a nearby thicket. Whoever follows into this hiding place will not know what to expect, how much strength the prey is still able to muster and how much resistance it may offer. If the animal still has enough reserves after all, for the hunter this could mean the risk of severe injury or even death. If the pack leader was forced to enter the thicket, this would be a disaster for the entire pack. The boss who has led the pack with acumen and circumspection through all the hardships of life would all of a sudden be missing. As a result, there would have to be fights to establish a new pecking order, which would spell the end to a structured and secure pack life, and the entire pack would descend into a deep biological crisis. For this reason it is not the pack leader enters the hiding place first, but a lower ranking 'scout'.

If he gets killed or badly injured, this has a far less significant impact on the whole pack system. This may sound brutal, but in a biological sense with regard to the survival of a social community, it's the only way.

If you want a good species-appropriate relationship with your dog, and he wants to walk through doors and gates first, then let him. He'll always be the first to get into the car anyway… The same goes for the statement: 'Your dog always has to be made to move if he is lying or standing in your way, in order to demonstrate clearly who's boss!' This is also inaccurate, as can easily be proved through observation. Pack leaders in the wild will walk through groups of sleeping pack members without necessitating them to get up and move out of the way. The bosses just walk around them, because anyone who constantly needs proof of his authority would surely not make a very self-assured boss. Every now and then it does happen that an adult dog will insist on a certain spot, but this has individual educational reasons and does not follow any principle. Above all it would not always be applied to the same pack member. If your dog is lying in your way, and you don't mind walking around him, you can carry on doing so without fear of losing authority.

Neck shaking and snout grip

Next let's look at the much discussed use of shaking by the neck and the snout grip as disciplinary measures. The shaking by the neck is often interpreted as 'shaking to death' or 'intention to kill', because allegedly this is how dog kill their prey. This impression, however, can only be based on very superficial observation, because a closer look reveals that the shaking is not used to kill the prey, but to minimise the risk of being bitten by the still living prey, i.e., the risk of sustaining more severe injuries.

Once the battered animal is no longer able to defend itself effectively, the final death bite ensues. Smaller prey such as mice don't require shaking because the first grip usually results in a severing of the spine. However, what can be observed is that this prey is shaken and thrown up in the air again and again after it is dead. This has a nutritional reason. A small prey such as a mouse is eaten whole, because it contains all the nutritional substances that a wild dog or wolf requires: creatine from the fur, meat, the giblets, including the all-important contents of the stomach and intestines, and finally the bones. In order make all of these more digestible, the dog mixes the ingredients together by shaking them. The throwing in the air, followed by shaking and often 'pre-chewing' makes the prey more digestible for the dog, as the nutrients are broken down better. The shaking by the neck is therefore not an intention to kill at all, or moreover, a shaking to death.

In the pack, the shaking by the neck is actually used as a disciplining method. It has a comprehensive spectrum and is adapted to the individual personality of the perpetrator. At the lower end it might involve a quick push with the nose in the direction of the neck, accompanied by a grumble, the next level might involve a proper shaking by the scruff of the neck, and finally even throwing the perpetrator on his back. Therefore from a behaviourist point of view a brief shaking by the scruff of the neck is a species-appropriate and indispensable method for disciplining.

This is in contrast with the snout grip, which is completely unsuitable for this sort of thing, even though it is often being promoted as such. It can be observed when puppies of the age of around ten weeks are begging for food. Up to this point they were used to mum or dad regurgitating food for them upon being nudged on the lips. But now a new stage in the little tykes' development begins.

They have to get used to looking after their food needs themselves, i.e., they are weaned. In order to convince them that this source of food has come to an end, the parents take the puppy's snout into theirs. The dog babies, having enjoyed a free-for-all attitude regarding the food issue up to now, experience being told off for the first time. This should not be seen as a genuine act of disciplining, but rather as a benign and loving gesture with a message: 'Sorry, my child, this is a thing of the past. The hard school of life and survival has now begun. From now on you will have to join the back of the queue, and eat what everyone else is having.'

From a behaviourist perspective, the snout grip is part of a set of social and tender communications, which are also creating trust. The father often takes the entire head of one of his offspring into his mouth, in order to demonstrate his attitude of benevolence and social nurture towards them. In wolf packs, the snout grip can be observed during a howling chorus, as well. The head of the pack raises his voice to gather his pack around him, in order to begin a collective ritual with the following meaning: 'We belong together and accept your position.' A moment later the pack members approach him, communicating their submission and appeasement via gestures and facial expression, and attempt to lick his snout. In response, the head of the pack briefly takes the individual family member's snouts in his mouth. This promotes the mutual acceptance in the pack community. The collective howling that follows has the important additional effect of letting neighbouring packs know that this pack is still functioning and where its boundaries are.

Neutral expression

Next I would like to describe an interesting behaviour that you might never have noticed like this before: the shaking. You all know what it looks like when your dog comes out of the water and shakes himself dry. However, you can frequently observe this behaviour without the dog having got in the least bit wet. Completely out of the bluely our dog starts to shake himself as if he had just emerged out of the water! A small example. We go to the dog park to give our dog a chance to cultivate his friendships, while getting enough exercise at the same time. He plays and sniffs, and everything is as it should be. Then in the distance, all of a sudden he notices two strange dogs who seem to be very interested in an object lying on the ground. Our dog runs towards the two dogs, in order to have a closer look. The closer he gets the more he slows down, and suddenly he stops altogether.

He has noticed that the two dogs have found something edible, but doesn't want to approach any further and risk a quarrel. He turns round and runs back towards us, but stops suddenly and shakes himself. What does he want to say by this? From a behaviourist perspective you can literally call this the 'shaking off' of an intention. He shakes off his intention to inspect the dogs and the object, and by shaking himself he demonstrates his neutral attitude and position to everyone in his environment. If your dog shakes himself in this manner, you know that he has just broken off an intended action, and that he will now turn to another activity. Another way the dog has at his disposal to

If the dog shakes himself in everyday situations, as if he had just come out of the water, he demonstrates to his environment that he has not carried out a planned action. He then shakes himself in order to demonstrate his new neutral expression. (Photo: Köppel)

express his neutral attitude is the forward stretch. This looks similar to an invitation to play, the difference being, that the legs aren't spread sideways but pushed out towards the front. The rear is only slightly elevated. The dog is expressing something like: 'I have no bad intentions.' This behaviour can be observed well when watching a group of several dogs, especially when one dog has taken time out and returns in order to reintegrate himself into the collective.

Sneezing as a destressing mechanism

Finally, I would like to explain to you a behaviour that dogs use to reduce stress and conflict: the sneeze. This kind of sneeze can clearly be distinguished from the warning sneeze that is used by dogs and wolves to alert the others to a potential danger. The warning sneeze is a brief muffled nasal sound in association with the respective body posture, and an intense stare in the direction of the perceived or real threat.

In contrast, the destressing sneeze sounds similar to our sneeze, a spontaneous sneeze that is caused by an irritation of the nasal lining. The typical body posture for this is neutral and not aiming anywhere in particular, with a slight bowing and shaking of the head.

I hope you'll have some fun watching your dog in a playful and interested manner, and discovering his many different forms of expression, which you've got to know a little better and which you are now able to interpret a little better as well.

(Photo: Brodmann)

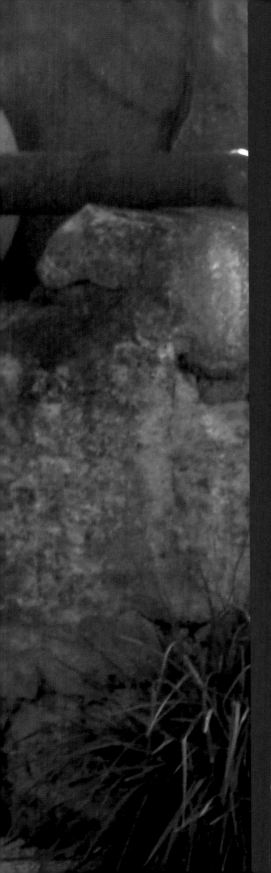

The final chapter

Yes, dear reader, you have already guessed it: this chapter is not just so named because it is the last one in this book, but also because it deals with the very final chapter of our friendship with our canine partner, the final farewell, death. I'm writing it because for me it belongs in this book as part of a species-appropriate life with our dog. The last stage of our path together ought to be species-appropriate and respectful.

(Photo: Krieger)

The laws of nature

Many people in our western society are determined to screen out death from their lives altogether. Even though death is looking over our shoulder day in, day out, it is persistently ignored. For some people, life consists of rushing from one appointment to the next, and from banquets to outlandish parties. Finding external peace is becoming increasingly difficult for 'the pinnacle of creation'. Maybe that's why so many people find it hard to find inner calm, as well. The words 'me', 'I want', 'I need', 'I own' have become more important than saying: 'I am only a tiny part of nature as a whole.'

Or, as my native American friends, the Lakota, as so-called Indians, would put it:

'Ehani maka iyuha caska na lila iyounkpipi.
Wamakaskan iyuha tanyan unpi.'

This roughly means:

'A long time ago all the land (life) was one, and we were happy.
The entire creation lived together in a good way.'

If we could see matters in this way, we would be able to accept nature and her laws, and with it the perpetual coming and going. Our friend deserves to die with dignity when his time has come. He should not have to suffer unnecessarily because we are projecting our fear of death on to him, because we think that with modern medical techniques we can outwit death. Let your dog go, even if it is hard. A dog doesn't want to die between sterile walls and under monstrous medical 'instruments of torture', but with you there, preferably on your lap.

A dog in the wild who feels that his life is nearing its end, either from old age or due to illness, submits to the ways of nature and prepares for 'eternal sleep'. He stops feeding and finds a suitable spot for dying. The pack just accepts this, and this is what the human pack should do, too.

A difficult decision

Some dog owners have the good fortune (if I may call it that) that their dog just passes away during the night. These people seem to have a direct line to the god of dogs. But most dog owners aren't spared the agonising decision at what point they should have their dog put to sleep. One thing is for certain, it is never a decision that is taken lightly. But as hard as it may seem, please make it before long, because our friend does not deserve to suffer unnecessarily.

Ask the vet to come to your home, so the inevitable can be done in familiar surroundings and doesn't needlessly create extra stress for your dog. If the vet turns you down, forget him for as long as you live, and stop greeting him in the street. A good vet will fulfil your request and put your dog to sleep in his familiar surroundings.

Close the door for the last journey with him. Pause for thought awhile, and look out of the window. You barely notice the wagon moving, and with your inner eye you begin to see images from a distant past with your dog. You lean back into your chair with a smile, because you are seeing your clumsy puppy in front of you, as he is about to find out the hard way that the glass door was closed after all. You are seeing the juvenile in his period of storm-and-stress, as he is emptying the bin, and you're seeing him walk like John Wayne at his next encounter with another dog. And so much more…

Now this old dog is lying on your lap on his very last journey with you, and at the end of this journey you are alone. The German singer Reinhard Mey has described this letting go so well that I'd like to relate a brief passage from it (and I hope that he'll forgive me for the added references to dogs):

The thought of the final farewell is part of the life you share with your beloved dog. (Photo: Brodmann)

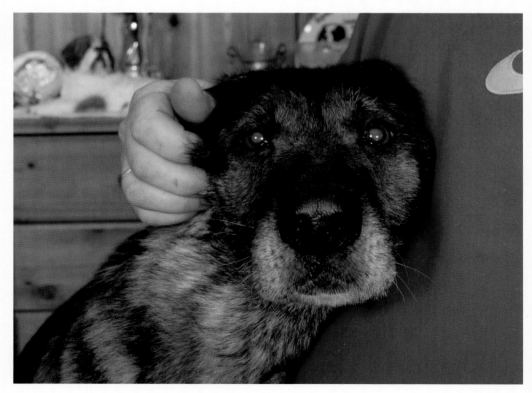

'The years are passing,
our time flies away.
We are turning in circles,
and this makes sense:
Everything must end and
make way for new things.
You, little puppy, are the morning,
and free as the wind!
Children and dogs have been
loaned to us but for a short time,
and they have come,
in order to move on.
But letting them go
is the hardest of lessons,
patience old dog,
I'm learning it now!
My old dog on my lap;
join in the dance,
I'm letting you go!'

(paraphrasing Reinhard Mey)

What's left are the memories

The memories and photographs remain, and perhaps there will be a naughty little tyke already waiting to become your old dog's successor.

But, as I've already said, before that it's saying farewell, and if at all possible, do it like this. Take your dog on your lap or lie next to him. He will enjoy these last minutes with you, if you stroke him in his favourite spot and gently cuddle him – and he will know at the same time that this is the end of his earthly existence. Calm and full of trust, he'll accept the injection. For the last time, he will feel the warmth and safety of your presence, and then he will just fall asleep.

(Photo: Köppel)

Even though all this is very hard, you will know that you have done the right thing. It is completely normal to be crying your eyes out now, otherwise you'd better forget about ever having another dog. In any case, it is a comforting thought that there is a 'dog heaven' after all!

If you have a garden or a plot of land, ask your local authority, whether you are allowed to bury your dog there. Perhaps you can give him his last bone, which he never managed to finish, and his favourite toy; he may find them useful on his journey. If you don't own a plot of land, there might be another solution. Surely you must have had a favourite place that you used to visit on your walks, where you may have liked to rest, or play with your dog. Ask the responsible authority or the gamekeeper, if this spot might become your dog's final resting place. Then this little place in nature will always remain special for you. And when you pass this spot with that clumsy little tyke of a successor, you can tell the tiny tot a few interesting stories about his predecessor...